Equip to Serve

100 WAYS TO HELP THE ONES YOU LEAD

ART BARTER & CAROL MALINSKI

Published by Wheatmark®
2030 East Speedway Boulevard, Suite 106
Tucson, Arizona 85719 USA
www.wheatmark.com

ISBN: 978-1-62787-761-9 (paperback)
ISBN: 978-1-62787-762-6 (hardcover)
ISBN: 978-1-62787-763-3 (ebook)
LCCN: 2020909952

Bulk ordering discounts are available through Wheatmark, Inc. For more information, email orders@wheatmark.com or call 1-888-934-0888.

Other books by Art Barter

▶ *Farmer Able: A Fable about Servant Leadership Transforming Organizations and People from the Inside Out*

▶ *The Servant Leadership Journal: An 18 Week Journey To Transform You and Your Organization*

▶ *The Art of Servant Leadership II: How You Get Results Is More Important Than the Results Themselves*

Contents

Acknowledgments

From Art Barter . . .

I would like to thank the team at Datron World Communications for their continued desire to serve others. These are your stories; stories which have had a profound impact on my life. The leadership team has participated, witnessed and survived my servant leadership transformation. Thank you for your servant's heart.

Thank you to the team at the Servant Leadership Institute for their work in helping to complete this book. I am blessed to work with a group of individuals who strive to inspire and equip others to become servant leaders. You are special people with great hearts. Your desire to help others is an inspiration. Ken Blanchard told me several years ago that it isn't what your team does when you're around, but what your team does when you're not there.....SLI is a great team!

My co-author, Carol Malinski, and I have worked together at Datron since 1997. I started at Datron as the VP of Finance and Operations. At that time, Carol was in charge of planning in manufacturing. We have experienced each other's transformation. Thank you, Carol, for your influence and impact on creating our culture of servant leadership at Datron. I am inspired by your desire to add value to others by leading from your heart. Thank you for taking on this project, doing most of the writing and editing, and blessing me through the process.

From Carol Malinski...

I could not have done this project or any other without support on the home front. To my husband, Joie, thanks for your strength and patience. And, thank you to my son Bryan, who supplied some of the photos for this book; I'm so blessed you caught the servant leadership bug.

During the last 25 years, I have been fortunate enough to be led by four individuals who developed and encouraged me; not only in my work, but more importantly supported me through the unfolding of my life's events. You all are real servant leaders and will have my gratitude forever: Roger Gillespie, Gary French, Robin Swift and Art Barter.

To all the people who have ever been part of the Datron and SLI families, all of you are extraordinary. Through your quiet efforts, you've positively impacted people all over the world. Thanks for letting me be part of the story.

Foreword

I'm so excited you picked up this book! When I first started working at the Servant Leadership Institute (SLI) over eight years ago, the most common question we were asked was: *what is servant leadership?* Today's most frequently asked question is: *how do you implement servant leadership?*

It's no coincidence that when a leader's mindset is not solely focused on their own self-interest (power leader), but instead on adding value to others (servant leader), most business measurements improve dramatically.

Today there is a growing demand for practical application instructions for implementing servant leadership. Art Barter, SLI's founder and CEO, effectively teaches servant leadership implementation through keeping the practical application simple and useful. Under Art's leadership, Carol Malinski, SLI's Director of Content and Curriculum, documents practical ways Art and his leadership team brought servant leadership to life at Datron World Communications. For example, here's a tip based on the use of small groups:

As Datron World Communications got into the process of culture transformation, we learned the power of using small groups to support the leadership team. These groups, made up of about 10 leaders, gather once or twice a month to share challenges and triumphs. The most important ground rule is "what is shared in the group, stays in the group" and that confidentiality is taken very seriously. There is no set agenda and no deliverables. Helping each other and learning to trust each other opens the door to stronger teams and problem-solving. The value of having a group of leaders you can share with and offer help to is priceless.

This week, think about how you might establish a small group or groups in your organization. If you are unable to allocate company time to this, see who is willing to meet during lunch once a month. It will be time well spent.

Each leadership lesson includes a challenge for you to sharpen your skills. I encourage you to pick one leadership lesson on a weekly basis, contemplate it, read it a few times, and then take on the challenge courageously! Share your results with your colleagues. In so doing, you'll be growing as a servant leader, increasing your influence and serving others.

Walking in the door every day with a mindset of *how I can bring value to others* may sound relatively easy to do. However, we are dealing with changing human behavior and that can get a bit complicated. I think you will appreciate the simplicity of this book, and the way it is filled with leadership ideas based on real life experiences from Art and Carol. The content of this book reflects thoughts and actions fostered by the cultural transformation at Datron World Communications. Art purchased Datron in 2004 and set about to transform the highly toxic manufacturing company to a servant led one. What evolved was a culture focused on serving the employees, customers, and community along with positive business results.

We've witnessed first-hand the evolution from confusion about servant leadership to the clarity that this leadership approach changes mindsets, and does indeed create the best leaders for the times by putting people first.

That's why I'm so happy you picked up this book.

Robin Swift
Past President, Servant Leadership Institute

An Introduction To Servant Leadership

BY ART BARTER

Servant leadership sounds like an oxymoron to some people. How can you lead people and be a servant at the same time? The truth is the two words work perfectly together when they are applied in their truest sense.

Leadership is influence pure and simple, but you can choose to be a "command and control" type leader or the kind of leader people want to follow. The Level 5 leader as defined by John Maxwell is the leader people follow simply because of the type of person that leader is. Leaders who care for their employees and their employees' families find people will go the extra mile and achieve results never thought possible.

Because leadership is influence, anyone can be a leader—but this is something you'll likely have to help your employees understand. Our culture has a tendency to only think of leaders as people with some sort of title. In truth, everyone is a leader. They influence others every day.

The word "servant" is actually derived from the French verb, "servir," to serve. It's a word that implies action, something we find very appropriate since servant leadership is all about behavior. How servant leaders behave should reflect a heartfelt need to add value to people.

The Servant Leadership Institute uses this definition: *Servant leadership is a set of principles and behaviors that turn the traditional "power" leadership model upside down, creating engaged, high performing people and a more caring world. As servant leaders, our purpose is to serve those who follow, to inspire and equip those we influence.* The key line in this definition is "to inspire and equip those we influence." When we inspire people we motivate, encourage and positively influence them. When we equip employees, we provide them with everything they need to accomplish their objectives and that includes training, equipment, setting expectations for them, as well as providing a healthy, safe work environment. If we do that, we will be leading at a higher level—for the sake of others.

At SLI, we like to describe what servant leadership is <u>not</u> because that helps people to understand what it is. Servant leadership is not related to your formal position or title. It can be practiced by anyone, anywhere and at any time. It's also not limited by your job description. If you have something to share—whether it's a specific skill or some pertinent information—do it. If you need information, ask for it. You don't need to ask permission to treat people with dignity and respect.

One of the biggest misconceptions about servant leadership is that it's soft, that people are never challenged or held accountable. Nothing could be further from the truth. If you truly care about your employees, you want to see them succeed. You want them to achieve great results because it's the results that keep a company operating. Servant leadership is actually the most difficult leadership practice, because you're constantly dealing with leading and changing human behavior. You must look at yourself deeply as well as those you lead to understand your mindset and whether you need to change your behavior to truly honor and serve others. Once you do, you can ask others to change with you.

How can you change your mindset from one of the power leader to one who serves? We believe mindset change occurs when we change our behaviors. The set of nine servant leader behaviors can easily become "the rules of the game" for your department or whole organization. Here they are, with a short description:

Serve First. This can be as simple as not always rushing to be the first one in the potluck line or as complex as sincerely examining your attitude as you approach each encounter. Am I going into this meeting wanting to control everything? Am I trying to run down another group to show my power or do I want to add value to the situation?

Build Trust. The most meaningful way you can build trust is to do what you say you're going to do. It's just that simple. If you make a commitment, you must keep it or renegotiate it. Maybe you're so busy in your job that you're often late to meetings or constantly rescheduling commitments—or you commit something and then just don't follow through. You allow this to occur because you think there's no consequence—but people don't trust you when these behaviors persist.

Live Your Values. Have you taken the time to figure out what your values are? Does your organization have values that are clearly stated for employees? Living your values means you make decisions with those values in mind. Decision-making becomes much easier with a clearly defined set of values to guide you and the organization to succeed.

Listen to Understand. Many leaders believe they're great listeners. As a servant leader, you continually evaluate your listening skills. "He/she never listens to me so why should I bother?" is the refrain of many employees. Do you start to listen but then jump in to interrupt because you feel you have the answer? Do you let others finish their thoughts? Listening to understand is a necessity for a servant leader. By making requests like "Tell me more" or "Help me understand", others will feel you truly want to listen.

Think About Your Thinking. Servant leaders become very

conscious about their own thinking in all interpersonal relationships. You must ask yourself important questions. "Am I willing to listen to honest feedback? Am I willing to consider my responsibility in any situation? How am I representing the mission and purpose of the organization? Am I displaying a positive attitude about it or am I one of the naysayers?" Servant leaders take what they hear and reflect on the potential improvements they need to make.

Add Value to Others. What do you think would happen if you entered every meeting with the mindset of wanting to add value to the situation? Imagine how much time you would save and how productive you could be if no one thought about having to "win" in the discussion. One of the ways we bring value is through our individual strengths, yet how many of us are encouraged to find out what those strengths are so they can bring value to others in the organization?

Demonstrate Courage. Are you willing to face a situation that's been on your mind for days, months or even years? Perhaps you have an employee with a behavioral issue who's adversely affecting your team, or a co-worker who continually runs down or gossips about the company. Have the courage to have the difficult conversation with that employee. Perhaps you recognize your own performance isn't what it should be and yet you continue your old behaviors. Have the courage to face your shortcomings and be transparent with your leader.

Increase Your Influence. We know leadership is influence and it can be exerted either positively or negatively. As a servant leader, part of your role in an organization is to spread your influence to add value. Your service should not be confined to just the group you work with; your influence can touch many areas in your organization, not to mention your customers and suppliers. Once service becomes your mindset, you'll approach everything in your life from the perspective of serving others to increase your positive influence.

Live Your Transformation. Living your transformation means your mindset has changed. You now interact with the world by asking, "How can I add value?" We like to say, "If you have something, share it, and if you need something, ask for it." There are no victims in a servant-led environment—only people who desire to contribute to one another's success. This is where everyone watches the leader to see if their behaviors and words are in sync.

These are the behaviors SLI believes can change our work environments, our communities, and most importantly those we love most in our lives.

There is so much that can be learned and read about servant leadership. These are the basics. This book is a compilation of mini scenarios you'll find in workplaces the world over. They're situations we've encountered and each one offers you an opportunity to consider it from a servant leader's perspective.

We invite you to read, reflect, write, and take action based on the challenges we offer. You'll never regret striving to be a better leader, one who treats everyone with dignity and respect. Servant leadership is a life-long journey—won't you join us on the road less traveled? It is a journey worth taking that will impact your life and the lives around you.

Enjoy your journey!

Build Trust

The other day, I delegated an especially important task to another team member. I have a tendency to be a "nervous Nelly" at times when delegating work. Yes, I am a work in progress as a servant leader. As I reflected on how best to check on the work but not appear to be distrustful, I had a small revelation. I was not doubting my teammate; I was questioning myself and whether or not I had fully prepared this person to do the task.

When you delegate work this week, remember to circle back to the person you gave the assignment to and ask this powerful question, "Have I fully equipped you to do this task?" A servant leader's mindset is to look at his or her own behavior first.

Ever done something that broke trust with someone else? We probably all have at one time or another. It's a lousy feeling and one that can eat at you until it's resolved. When it happens at work, there are some steps you can take to restore trust.

Trust can be broken quickly, but it can only be rebuilt slowly. Apologize for your part in the situation. When trust is broken, words can't always help, but actions can—so be consistent keeping your commitments going forward. Do what you said you would do.

_____

_____

_____

_____

_____

_____

_____

_____

_____

_____

_____

_____

_____

_____

_____

_____

Trust is at the core of servant leadership. Leadership is a position of trust and responsibility. Trust is voluntary and cannot be forced. It's a choice we make and a risk we take.

As you are faced with deciding whether to extend trust, be aware that when you trust, you are letting part of your life go and be put into the hands of another—accepting a position of vulnerability. Great leaders are willing to be vulnerable.

_____

_____

_____

_____

_____

_____

_____

_____

_____

_____

_____

_____

_____

_____

_____

_____

_____

All of us have situations every day where we must trust someone else. In some cases, it's easy to do. For example, you board an airplane and trust the pilot knows how to fly it. You go to the doctor and trust he or she will know how to cure your ailments. Why is it so hard to extend trust in the workplace? If you want to build trust, you must be willing to extend trust.

Extend trust to someone at work. That means:

- **You trust their commitments to you till they prove untrustworthy.**

- **You don't double check their work.**

- **You freely give them information they need.**

Be courageous—they're not airline pilots, so what do you have to lose?

_____

_____

_____

_____

_____

_____

_____

_____

_____

_____

Want to build the trust in your team? Learn to delegate the work that must be done. Yes, loosen your death grip on those file folders and task lists and look at the situation with new eyes. Who else on the team can do this task successfully? Can you think of a better way to show you trust your team's ability than delegating work to them?

Try delegating using these six steps as a guideline to delegation.

    1. Communicate the task. (what, when, and end result)

    2. Furnish context. (explain the "why" and possible challenges)

    3. Determine standards. (e.g., what a home run looks like)

    4. Grant the authority.

    5. Provide support. (a servant leader equips the team)

    6. Get commitment. (confirm expectations)

_____

_____

_____

_____

_____

_____

_____

_____

_____

_____

Have you ever wondered if the people you influence trust you? Stephen M.R. Covey, world-renowned expert on trust, has said "nothing is as fast as the speed of trust and people can get good at creating it." Do you speak truthfully with no spin? Do you do what you say you're going to do?

Periodically, ask your group three questions (making names optional). Do you trust your boss? Do you trust management? And do you trust your co-workers? It may be an eye-opening experience.

_____

_____

_____

_____

_____

_____

_____

_____

_____

_____

_____

_____

_____

_____

_____

_____

_____

Communication

At some point in your working life, you have probably sat in an all-employee meeting. The purpose of these meetings is to communicate the state of the organization or any number of topics. As the executive speaks, do you ever wonder if people understand what the heck he is talking about? Many employees don't understand financial charts and graphs or accounting terms like ROI or operating profit vs revenue.

As a leader, this is a time to exercise the power of the question. If the speaker takes questions from the audience, ask some, even if you know the answers. Other people may have the same questions, but they're afraid to ask. In a servant-led environment, we want everyone to understand what's going on with the company. So, ask some good questions; other people will be glad you did.

Call me a slow learner, but it was not until the last decade of my 30 years in business that I have come to appreciate the use of questions in communicating. Getting your point across by using questions seems to diffuse possibly emotional conversations and unify teams—and they can make people feel like problems are being solved together.

The next time you're in a difficult conversation with someone over a plan of action, try using clarifying questions to define it. Instead of declarations like, "I think we should do _____," try a question like, "Do you think it might work better if we _____" or "Is there a way we could reach our desired outcome by_____."

_____

_____

_____

_____

_____

_____

_____

_____

_____

_____

_____

_____

_____

_____

_____

Working with a team of people can be a real adventure. It can be particularly challenging if there are no guidelines established dictating how team members behave with one another. Ground rules is a principal we teach in our servant leadership training curriculum. It is basically a communications contract that states how the team will work together.

Next time you're establishing a work team, have a discussion right at the beginning of the project focused on how you will work together. Ground rules might include:

- **We will be on time to meetings.**

- **We will not interrupt each other when talking.**

- **We will finish meetings on time.**

You can use servant leadership behaviors as guideposts. Now when people don't respect the rules you established as a team, all you need to say is "ground rules!" to bring the team back on track.

What's a three-letter word that can demoralize a whole room of people? It's the tiny word "but."

"You did a good job, but…"

"What you've written is very interesting, but…"

"I love you, but…"

Does anyone like that word? As servant leaders, we're here to inspire and equip—not to deflate people.

This week, when you're tempted to use the word "but," substitute the word "and" whenever you can as you seek to influence people. For example:

"You did a good job and I think we can enhance the project by…"

"What you've written is very interesting and I think you can explore…"

"I love you, and I know we can get better together."

Let's stamp out that negative little three-letter word!

_____

_____

_____

_____

_____

_____

_____

_____

Are you passionate about the purpose of your company? How about the purpose of your department within the organization? No matter what you make or what service you provide, your work has meaning and purpose; sometimes, you just have to work to find it. As a servant leader, it's your job to find it, communicate it and fulfill it with your team.

Communicate regularly with your direct reports about how their activities are fulfilling the company purpose. Help people understand why their performance makes a difference—not only why they do something, but how they do it matters.

_____

_____

_____

_____

_____

_____

_____

_____

_____

_____

_____

_____

_____

_____

Command decisions are part of a leader's life. One of the misconceptions about servant leadership is that every decision must be made by a group and command decisions no longer have a place in the organization. This is simply not true. There will be times when a command decision must be made to move the organization forward. How you do it is what matters to servant leaders.

When making a command decision, ask yourself what your motive is. It should be based on what is best for the organization, not what is best for individuals. Remember to communicate why you're making the decision as soon as possible. This communication can be used as a teaching moment so next time, the team will be better equipped to make the decision without you.

Have you been known to stretch or bend the truth? Are there instances where you present information slanted in a way that shows you or your team in a better light than what's true? Servant leaders strive for transparency in all their interactions. Good decisions can't be made unless they are based on accurate information. Every organization must generate results, but let's be careful how we get them.

Pay special attention to how you are giving information to others. Be completely straightforward with the data you present. Put all your cards "face up" on the table. You will be known as a person of integrity and that is a great thing to be!

What does the word "lead" mean to you? To guide, show the way and influence all come to mind. Some people don't feel they're leaders unless they have some kind of management title. The truth is, everyone is a leader somewhere, sometime.

This week, have a conversation with the people you lead to help them understand they are leaders—whether they're managing a team, serving as a soccer coach, or being a mom or dad. Because they're leaders, it's important they speak and act in ways worth following.

_____

_____

_____

_____

_____

_____

_____

_____

_____

_____

_____

_____

_____

_____

_____

_____

As you are working on building a servant-led culture, you may find it difficult to build the necessary mindset in your team. People are busy doing their jobs and may not have the time or the awareness to think deeply about how they might serve one another. It may be a real challenge to move the needle beyond just being nice to one another.

If you have a regular status meeting with your team, add an element of story-telling. Ask people to share their stories that illustrate servant leadership. At first this will be difficult for people, so come prepared with a story to share. But as time goes on, people will feel more comfortable and the stories will become part of the fabric of your new culture.

Most of us who lead departments have regular meetings with our teams to discuss status of deliverables and all the little details involved in meeting our goals. But servant leaders inspire and equip the people they influence. That means we can also use this time for teachable moments. Why not share what you have learned about servant leadership with your team?

Each week, dedicate 10 to 20 minutes to teach a servant leader behavior to your team during your staff meeting. Don't forget SLI has resources on our website for you to use. It's just another way you can influence the team to serve each other first. You'll be glad you showed the way.

_____

_____

_____

_____

_____

_____

_____

_____

_____

_____

_____

_____

_____

_____

_____

It's no secret that five generations are now represented in our workplaces. It seems as though this would be a marvelous opportunity for the more experienced people to share their vast knowledge and expertise, but is that really happening? We have one client who told us they have a serious issue with their older engineers not sharing information with their younger colleagues. This goes on in many workplaces and not just among the generations. Do you really believe sharing information will cause you to lose your job? Do you really want to carry this information into retirement with you?

This week, do everyone a favor and when you have information others need, share it with them. Look for opportunities to help people in this way. They will appreciate it and you'll gain a reputation for adding value.

_____

_____

_____

_____

_____

_____

_____

_____

_____

_____

_____

_____

I once had a boss who had no leadership heart or skill. If I made a mistake, she would come absolutely unglued. If I didn't do things exactly the way she did, I was automatically wrong. What happened as a result was I made even more mistakes—because I was so afraid to make an error. She could not see the potential in me because she had no vision or desire to mentor me.

This week, as your team members are challenged by work tasks, they will make mistakes. As you mentally prepare to mentor and correct the missteps, keep in mind their potential and communicate from that perspective. The counseling session will be a much more positive experience as you correct the unacceptable behavior while reaffirming your faith in them.

Power-driven leaders love to give orders. Their attitude is, "just do your job and don't ask questions." A servant leader, on the other hand, will take the time to explain the bigger picture of why a certain task needs to be done. Servant leaders will paint the bigger picture to motivate and engage employees.

As you assign work, tell the bigger story of why it's important. Tie it to your mission and values. Team members will appreciate knowing the why behind the what, and trust will be built.

_____

_____

_____

_____

_____

_____

_____

_____

_____

_____

_____

_____

_____

_____

_____

_____

_____

_____

As a leader, do you feel strongly that certain tasks should be done a certain way? Have you ever wondered why the outcome of a project is not what you'd envisioned even though you feel you were so clear in your instructions? A servant leader's role is to equip their team in every possible way. Clarifying expectations is a vital part of equipping people. Our teams should understand what the deliverable should be and if how they get there is important or not.

As you delegate work or projects, describe exactly what you want done, when you want it complete, what the end result should look like and why it's important. If the work needs to be done in a certain way, explain that too. Your goal should be to never hear the phrase, "I didn't understand the task (or project)."

_____

_____

_____

_____

_____

_____

_____

_____

_____

_____

_____

_____

_____

Connection and Relationship

A servant leader connects with people. Your job as a leader is to make a real connection with those you influence. A leader shared with us once, "I never realized getting to know the people in my group was part of my job." It may not be written in our corporate job descriptions, but it certainly should be. Connecting with those you lead is not something you do when all the other work is done. We suggest you make it part of your daily calendar. Some leaders like to proudly proclaim, "I have an open door policy," when in fact no one is brave enough to walk through their door. Be aware that you have the power to change the environment.

Make a connection each day this week; you'll be glad you did.

If you're like me, you never seem to get caught up on all the reading you'd like to do. Between your job, your home life, and your hobbies, time to read and learn new things is hard to come by. But servant leaders are lifelong learners, so here's an idea to fit reading into your lifestyle and into your team.

Choose a leadership audio book or one on some other appropriate subject like time management and schedule 45 minutes a week for a meeting where you listen to it. Dedicate 10-15 minutes to discuss what stood out for you. Some of you may object to taking this time away from "work." I get it. If that's your situation, see if you can get colleagues to meet at lunchtime once a week for 45 minutes to listen and discuss. You'll love the new thoughts, the sense of accomplishment and the relationship-building.

_____

_____

_____

_____

_____

_____

_____

_____

_____

_____

_____

_____

Ever have the feeling that your work life revolves around email? Like many of us, you probably could spend your entire workday focused on two things: email and meetings. But beyond those commitments is a whole other job you need to do.

I'd like to propose a couple things you can do to break out of the email spell:

- **If you're emailing someone who's in your office within walking distance, don't. Get up from your desk and have a face-to-face conversation.**

- **Really think about who you're copying to ensure only those who "need to know" are included. And don't "reply all" without thinking first.**

Let's practice things to control email and not allow it to control us.

_____

_____

_____

_____

_____

_____

_____

_____

_____

_____

Do your team members understand what you expect of them? In many workplaces, new hires are handed a job description and trained in the details of how to do their job. But we seldom train people about how we expect them to do business with one another. We don't spell out our expectations for how we interface with one another or with clients or suppliers.

Begin to have conversations with your team about your group's code of conduct. You can use the 9 Behaviors of a Servant Leader (email us at info@servantleadershipinstitute.com for a digital copy) or have your team members come up with their own list of behavioral expectations. This will build their ownership of the process.

_____

_____

_____

_____

_____

_____

_____

_____

_____

_____

_____

_____

_____

_____

Have you ever reported to a leader who seemed to speak an entirely different language than you? I have and it was a painful experience where I was often frustrated. I'm sure my boss wondered how I'd ever achieved my position. In came servant leadership to the rescue. When we began to talk as people, not caring about our roles in the organization, something wonderful happened. We started speaking the same language and communication greatly improved. Even taking constructive feedback became easier for me.

Is there someone in your organization you just can't seem to get on the same page with? Make an effort to find common ground. Try going for coffee, lunch or even a walk around the building together. Don't even talk business; just get to know each other. Your communication is bound to improve.

Want to build the relationships between members of your team? Sometimes it takes some intervention to really bring teams together to work more cohesively and literally as a team. Here's an idea brought to us by a very sharp engineering V.P.

During your staff meetings, arrange some time for team members to share about their lives with one another. Ask them to prepare a little presentation emphasizing what they do away from work. Make it voluntary and you might go first to start the ball rolling. You'll find out the most interesting things about each other and it will go a long way toward bringing the team together.

Have a new employee coming on board? How prepared are you? When you have a new person in your group, your focus is often introducing them to department personnel and training them—and you're done. But as a servant leader, you want to inspire and equip each individual and that means helping them assimilate successfully into the company as a whole.

Next time you have a new employee starting in your group, assign them a "buddy" to help them get settled. Make sure someone asks them to lunch. And schedule time for them to visit with each department they'll be interfacing with, upstream and downstream. The sooner they understand how the organization flows, the more successful they'll be.

As Datron World Communications entered the process of culture transformation, we learned the power of using small groups to support the leadership team. These groups, made up of about 10 leaders, gather once or twice a month to share challenges and triumphs. The most important ground rule is "what is shared in the group, stays in the group" and that confidentiality is taken very seriously. There is no set agenda and no deliverables. Helping each other and learning to trust each other opens the door to stronger teams and problem-solving. The value of having a group of leaders you can share with and offer help to is priceless.

Think about how you might establish a small group or groups in your organization. If you are unable to allocate company time to this, see who is willing to meet during lunch once a month. It will be time well spent.

Most of us have people we work with who we really don't have a relationship with. We talk to them because we must get work done. When we need their help, at times it is almost like they are an adversary, not a teammate working for the same end goal. Servant leaders seek to build connections with all the people they work with. The result is a working environment where people care about one another and better work gets done.

Over the next week, take a look around at those you interface with. Who do you know very little about? Who leads an area you don't really understand? For me it was Finance. Ask that person to have a cup of coffee with you (maybe even once a week) so you can get to know them better. Tell them you'd like to understand their world. What you will find is if you build that relationship, you are no longer adversaries; now you are work friends, helping one another achieve excellent results.

Servant leaders are on a mission to build relationships with the people they influence. One way to do this is to schedule weekly One-on-One meetings with your direct reports. And don't just talk about work assignments; find out what's important to them. What are their hobbies? What are their kids up to? What things would they love to do for the organization? What are their long-term goals? How can you help them achieve those goals? When something comes up that interferes with your One-on-Ones, and inevitably it will, make sure to reschedule as soon as possible. People want to know you are serious about spending that time with them.

It's been said, "People don't care how much you know till they know how much you care." Servant leaders build positive relationships with others. Make a One-on-One part of your calendar today.

As you walk the halls of your workplace, acknowledge the people you pass. I know this may sound very elementary, but we have heard employees in companies tell us "so and so walks right by us and never even says 'hi.'" Canadian leadership consultant Olivia McIvor notes, "You have a beautiful smile. Don't forget to tell your face." When you ignore people as you pass by, they take it personally. You build walls that will be hard to tear down.

This week, acknowledge every person you pass by and if you really want to be bold, greet them with your best smile!

_____

_____

_____

_____

_____

_____

_____

_____

_____

_____

_____

_____

_____

_____

_____

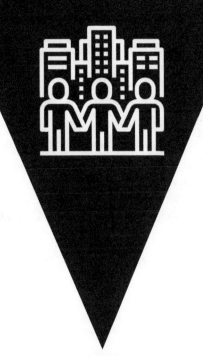

Culture

At SLI, we say servant leadership is to inspire and equip those we influence. Leaders must equip their teams with everything they need to be successful and that includes having the right tools to use—be it a computer or a power screwdriver. Howard Behar, former CEO of Starbucks, has said, "If you want someone to mop the floor, let them choose the mop."

Next time you are ready to equip someone with a tool of some kind, let them choose it. Who knows better what is needed for the job? Your team will appreciate being able to be involved in the decision!

_____

_____

_____

_____

_____

_____

_____

_____

_____

_____

_____

_____

_____

_____

_____

_____

Ever make your job bigger or more complicated than it really needs to be? I have observed this situation is quite common and reveals itself only when employees move out of a position and someone else begins to do their work. This situation comes out of a need, warranted or not, to protect our position within the organization. In many organizations, there is a constant fear we will lose our place, so many folks add extra steps or layers to processes to show everyone how invaluable they are.

Servant leaders should be on a campaign to create a workplace where people don't have to be frightened. We need workplaces where people are not afraid to speak up if they don't have enough work to do. When we design processes to run our businesses, every employee should be looking to implement the most efficient and effective method to fulfill the company mission and purpose.

_____

_____

_____

_____

_____

_____

_____

_____

_____

_____

_____

_____

Servant leadership is about creating environments where people can be kind to one another. I know it sounds corny, but given a choice, wouldn't you rather work in a place where people are kind? That doesn't mean we don't correct people when they fall short, but we do it while showing respect for the individual. Kindness creates safety, and people want to feel safe when they go to work. It's just that simple.

Olivia McIvor, a researcher, HR professional and expert on kindness in the workplace, is determined to spread kindness throughout the world. She teaches that, "Kindness is simple. Before you speak or take action, ask yourself three questions: Is it truthful? Is it necessary? Is it kind?"

_____

_____

_____

_____

_____

_____

_____

_____

_____

_____

_____

_____

_____

Ever felt left out or left behind at work because of your age? Whether you're a Gen Z, millennial or boomer, the situation can arise where you feel you've been set aside or discounted. It's not a good feeling, especially when you know you have ideas to contribute. Each generation has qualities that are valuable and as a leader, it's up to you to find those strengths and take advantage of them. Don't fall prey to stereotypes.

Make room for all generations at the conference room table—and offer not just a seat, but a "say." Servant leaders serve everyone, not just those who think exactly the way they do or have the same approach to work. When contributions are welcome from everyone, our organizations will be better.

I once had an individual share with me that at his company, everyone had to agree on a decision before it was made. As you can imagine, things did not move very rapidly due to the need for that level of consensus. These people believed that in a servant-led organization, you always had to have complete accord.

On the contrary, even in a servant-led organization, there are times when a command decision is made. When timelines are tight, when you alone are informed, and when you have the respect of the team and the authority to make the decision—make it. It's very important, though, to explain to team members why you did what you did; doing so will be a learning experience and better prepare them for future decision-making.

Do you or your team members call a cubicle home from 8:00 to 5:00? No matter what your physical work space looks like, you're probably experiencing lots of chatter and various discussions that don't really involve you. It can be a challenge right? Maybe you don't really care what Sally had for dinner last night or what kind of problems she is having in her relationship. As a servant leader, your responsibility is to equip people to be able to concentrate and be successful at their jobs. That means you provide the best working environment possible.

If this is an issue for you and your team, it's time for ground rules. Call the team together with the purpose of creating the rules of behavior in the office. Things like keeping voices down in the cubicle area, even acceptable language should be discussed and agreed upon. If the team takes ownership of ground rules, it is far more likely that the culture will improve and you won't have to be the policeman.

When you have a position to fill, do you know what are you looking for in an employee? Many times, we have a specific position we need to fill and we look for people who have done that job in the past. It's the most direct way to fill our need. But what about all the "other" things we need in an employee—the qualities that may not be found on that job description.

Ask your team for input on this and create a description of your expectations for a member of your team. This will come in handy when you are looking to fill a position.

_____

_____

_____

_____

_____

_____

_____

_____

_____

_____

_____

_____

_____

_____

There is a very prevalent sickness that goes on in our workplaces called "victim-itis." One symptom is a lack of action because you are waiting for someone else to give you information so you can do your job. Another is whining about how you can't get the information you need because another person or group is not paying attention to your needs. Thankfully, this is a curable disease and in fact is quite preventable. Simply encourage your team members to ask for what they need.

This week, focus on watching for "victim-itis." When you see it going on, influence the people involved to step out of their departments and ask for what they need. In the process, they will learn more about the work flow in another group and find new and better ways to work together. Team members will learn they are brave enough and strong enough to not be victims anymore.

_____

_____

_____

_____

_____

_____

_____

_____

_____

_____

_____

_____

_____

There are now five generations working in our businesses. Are we working together? Or do we continue to gain satisfaction from pointing out our differences? I have attended more than one speaking event where the "expert" spent time making jokes at the expense of Millennials. Servant leadership requires valuing everyone—and that means looking for what we have in common rather than taking pleasure in complaining about our differences.

Look at the demographics of the people you work with and serve. Examine the group's values and goals and find the common threads. These will be the foundation you can begin to build on to create a rich, productive work group.

_____

_____

_____

_____

_____

_____

_____

_____

_____

_____

_____

_____

_____

Do you hear your team talking about other teams they interface with in a negative way? Is your company caught up in an "us versus them" culture? Some years ago, the supervisor in a department I led came up with a great idea: a department exchange. She scheduled time with each department our group interfaced with to have an informational get-together. In these meetings, each department explained what it does, described its challenges, and what it needed from us and why. Together, we looked for ways to improve our communication with each other.

Look at your upstream and downstream customers and choose one department to meet with. Focus on building relationships as well as process improvement. Remember two things: no finger-pointing and bring some goodies to share!

_____

_____

_____

_____

_____

_____

_____

_____

_____

_____

_____

_____

Avoid gossip within your sphere of influence and try to stop it whenever you can. This is a huge task and difficult to achieve, but just think how much more we could accomplish when we declare a "no-gossip" zone in the workplace.

Fight gossip by asking people direct questions when they pass along a tidbit that falls into that category. "Is talking about this useful to our thinking and what we are trying to accomplish?"

If I asked you to describe your workplace, you probably would not use words like steady, calm, logical or peaceful. It would be much more likely to hear words like fast-paced, frequently changing or even chaotic. The servant leader needs to be the one who keeps their cool, the one who maintains a non-anxious presence amid the storm. People need someone to go to when it may seem like the sky is falling. Running around like Chicken Little from the children's story proclaiming "the sky is falling! the sky is falling!" will do more harm than good.

When things get chaotic, close your door or retreat into your cubicle for a few minutes to breathe deeply and calm yourself. Practice some positive self-talk. Take a walk around the building if necessary. This week, practice maintaining the non-anxious presence people crave. You will serve people well if you do.

There is a culture of "lateness" that exists in many companies. The meeting is scheduled for 9 a.m. and people start moseying in around 9:10-ish. What does that say about the importance of the meeting? What is the message it sends to the person hosting the meeting? Do you think they might feel diminished? Being consistently late sends the message that the only person who matters is you. Servant leaders commit to honoring other people and believe everyone's time is valuable.

Be on time to every meeting and if that is not possible, communicate to the organizer that you will be late and why. Being on time will help you build trust with everyone you influence.

Demonstrate
Courage

At times, we all experience conflict in our work environments. Usually, someone disagrees with you and you both withdraw in a huff and talk about each other to anyone willing to listen.

Wouldn't it be healthier to do some on-the-spot conflict management? Ask your boss or another trusted person to lead you both through a process that will allow you to live in the other person's point of view for a few minutes.

- **Listen to the other person's point of view without interruption.**

- **Summarize what you hear to the other person's satisfaction. Reverse and repeat the process.**

- **Have your facilitator ask if listening has given you any new information or understanding. Work on ideas for resolving the conflict.**

_____

_____

_____

_____

_____

_____

_____

_____

_____

_____

_____

Early in my career, I made a serious mistake. The consequences would be costly and it was a "he said, she said" type of incident. I went to my boss to explain the situation, expecting to get help of some kind. What I got was a response I have never forgotten. As her chin quivered in anger, she said, "Well! What do you expect me to do about it?" I was not expecting her to fix it, but I was expecting some kind of moral support or perhaps an offer to help me work on a recovery plan.

As a servant leader, do you "have the backs" of the people who report to you? This doesn't mean you rescue them from all the tough situations or solve their problems for them. But it is your responsibility to lead them in learning how to solve their own problems.

_____

_____

_____

_____

_____

_____

_____

_____

_____

_____

_____

_____

_____

Ever had an employee on your team who always seems to have one personal problem after another? Perhaps it's affecting their attendance at work. You believe in servant leadership and you care about this person. I have seen companies bend over backwards and spend significant amounts of money to help employees. When is enough, enough?

As servant leaders, we want to help people through their life situations, but let's make sure we look at the full scope of the situation. Let's ask ourselves:

- **Is this situation affecting everyone in the group? Probably yes.**

- **Are other employees affected by this situation? They are watching.**

- **Is this an employee who needs a hand and then will be able to stand on their own? Help them.**

- **Does this person continue to behave in way that will only repeat the crisis?**

Sometimes you must make the tough decision and follow your process to remove this employee. You're not cold and heartless. You're responsible for the good of the whole team. Will you be a servant leader to one...or a servant leader to all?

_____

_____

_____

_____

_____

_____

How do you approach reporting your results on projects for which you are responsible? When reporting status, are you completely honest? Or do you slant your information just a bit so you look better? Are you willing to admit you may be struggling in some area of a project?

Servant leaders put all their cards face up on the table. When you report status, take a chance, be honest and ask for help if you need it. Encourage your fellow leaders to do the same and you just might change a culture!

How many of us are doing our jobs because we need to pay the bills? Probably quite a few. How many of us were challenged to find our gifts, do those things and get paid for it? Not too many, I would wager. As a servant leader, if you want to serve those you influence, you will help them find their gifts, the things that bring them joy, the things they were meant to do.

Take a risk this week; ask the people you lead to tell you what really makes them happy. If they don't know their gifts and talents, take them through a book or assessment tool that will help your team members find them. Then try to put them in roles where they can exercise those gifts.

_____

_____

_____

_____

_____

_____

_____

_____

_____

_____

_____

_____

_____

All of us have worked in situations where problems arise. I am not talking about fires that must be put out immediately, but those pesky problems that come up time and time again. Normally, we call together the team members in the department affected and discuss how we might change a process to resolve the issue. Do we ever question the makeup of these problem-solving teams? Maybe we need to expand our thinking and include some folks from other departments who might have insight on the issue. What other areas might this problem affect?

The next time there is a problem caused by weak or faulty processes, really think about who might add value to the process of finding a solution. Look upstream, downstream and across functions for contributors. You might find a whole new world of possibilities.

Apologies are powerful things, don't you agree? In a business setting when a leader says, "I'm sorry," it makes a lasting impression on employees; you'll climb 10 points on the likeability scale and increase trust. Servant leaders show they truly care when they're able to sincerely admit they were wrong and show their humanity by apologizing.

Do you need to apologize to a co-worker or direct report today? Is there someone in your personal life who deserves an apology for something you did or neglected to do? Show some courage—say "I'm sorry" this week.

Accountability is accepting responsibility for results. Servant leadership accountability involves holding ourselves and others accountable.

Give some thought to a project you may be working on or even leading.

Hold yourself accountable by:

- **Taking ownership for the situation**

- **Taking responsibility for results, good or bad**

- **Not blaming others when things go wrong**

- **Finding opportunities to act as a role model**

- **Requesting frequent feedback**

_____

_____

_____

_____

_____

_____

_____

_____

_____

_____

_____

_____

_____

_____

Servant leadership accountability involves holding ourselves and others accountable. We've shared about holding **ourselves** accountable. Now let's focus on holding **others** accountable.

Give some thought to a project you are leading.

Hold others accountable by:

- **Setting clear expectations for the team and individuals**

- **Teaching people to own the situation and problems**

- **Encouraging people to continually ask "what else can I do?"**

- **Allowing people to self-evaluate**

- **Giving feedback when individuals act as victims, blaming others**

- **Giving positive feedback and reinforcement for demonstrations of accountability**

_____

_____

_____

_____

_____

_____

_____

_____

_____

_____

Constructive feedback can answer the question, "What's it like to be on the other side of me?" Do you have a mentor or good friend who can give you constructive feedback about the wake you leave behind when you exit the room?

As a servant leader who wants to get better:

- **Be willing to hear the feedback.**

- **Recognize that feedback is a gift.**

- **Know you can change your behavior by adopting a serve-first mindset.**

_____

_____

_____

_____

_____

_____

_____

_____

_____

_____

_____

_____

_____

_____

Many people believe servant leadership is all about being nice, not really caring about the bottom line, but focusing on making sure everyone comes together to sing Kumbaya. That's far from the case—because if we really care about our employees, we want them to be successful and we want the company to thrive so employees stay employed!

Do you have a tracking system of some kind to help people be accountable? It can be as simple as an Excel spreadsheet of projects and tasks or as complex as a software tool that tracks project status. The important thing is having a mechanism through which employees can show accountability to their commitments.

Hold your team accountable – because you care!

Increase Your Influence

The word "mindset" is defined as an attitude, disposition or mood. A leader's mindset is critically important. In leadership, your mindset can be one of power or one of service.

The power mindset can be demonstrated by thinking about and treating employees as tools to get the job done. They strive to "make the numbers" every quarter, even if it means doing things in a "sketchy" way. A company I worked for many years ago used to ship product off the dock and then bring it back the day after month end. That way, it could increase the shipment numbers for the quarter.

A service mindset is grounded in integrity. A servant leader will support his people and not involve them in shady business practices. Because this leader shows high regard for the people he leads, his employees will strive to achieve better and better results. For the servant leader, the quest is not for personal power, but rather to meet the needs of others.

If you want to build a service mindset, ask yourself these questions:

What do people need? How can I help them get it?

What does my organization need to do? How can I help my organization do it?

_____

_____

_____

_____

_____

_____

_____

Do you rely on your title to influence others? It seems only natural that you would influence using your title when your whole culture is dedicated to showing deference to those with a title: president, CEO, movie star. You probably feel you have earned your title through hard work; I get it. But, it's really what you do with your title that counts. Is it used to intimidate? Is it used to ensure you get what you want at the expense of others? Do your employees use titles to get what they want?

It's time to abandon the notion that you are the top of the power pyramid. Every position in an organization is worthy of respect. By placing your ego at the bottom of the pyramid, you have the "power" to serve each and every person you place above you. Servant leadership is a mindset change.

_____

_____

_____

_____

_____

_____

_____

_____

_____

_____

_____

_____

_____

Can you determine your top five personal values? Now that you know your values, how do they line up against your company's values? Do you know your company's values? Are they a part of everyday life in your organization? Or do they simply occupy some wall space on a lovely plaque?

If we want to build servant-led organizations, it's time to take the values off the wall and make them a part of the culture of the company. Start to talk about them in team meetings and with individuals. Use them when evaluating performance and making decisions. Make them come alive for people and watch positive change begin to take place!

_____

_____

_____

_____

_____

_____

_____

_____

_____

_____

_____

_____

_____

Have you created an environment in your department or organization where "families first" is not only talked about, but is a part of your culture? When our working days are over, will we be surrounded by healthy, fulfilling relationships? That doesn't just happen; it takes commitment. That means if your phone rings and it's a family member, you answer the call—even in the middle of that "oh so important" meeting. It also means you practice a healthy work/life balance. And you make time to be a soccer mom or the team coach.

Do you have someone on your team who is struggling with a family situation? This week, ask them if they need some time to take care of the problem and allow them to take it. Make "family comes first" a reality. How can we all create a better work/life balance?

You lead a great team of people and things seem to be humming along. The group is providing value, getting things done in a timely manner and achieving good accuracy. Have you told them so? How often do you say, "good job!"? Are you finding ways to acknowledge what the team is accomplishing? Some people feel they don't need to praise someone for doing their job. I believe everyone likes to get an "atta boy" or "atta girl" from time to time.

This week, acknowledge someone's performance by giving them a greeting card that praises their effort. Want to strengthen your team? Encourage the group to give cards to one another when they witness effort that's above and beyond. You'll see some smiles, I guarantee it.

_____

_____

_____

_____

_____

_____

_____

_____

_____

_____

_____

_____

_____

_____

_____

"Thank you." These two little words do so much good in the world. Some leaders believe when people accomplish things, they are simply doing what they were hired to do, so expressing gratitude is not necessary. But a servant leader recognizes people for their accomplishments and values the contributions of the people they lead. Gratitude is an attitude that can be contagious.

Make it a point to say a sincere "thank you" to someone each day this week for the work they have accomplished. It will be a gift to both of you.

Gratitude—what does it have to do with our work? How does it impact our leadership? Gratitude is noun that implies action to me. To be effective in our work and in our leadership, having an attitude of gratitude makes a huge difference in how we look at the people we influence. When I find things or qualities to be grateful for in my team, it will change the way I view them and renew my belief about their ability to achieve success.

Start a new behavior. Before you reach the office or jobsite, think of three things you are grateful for about your team and say them out loud to yourself. Then take the next step and tell people what you are grateful for about them: "I'm grateful for the way you handled that phone call" or "I appreciate how you helped your teammate accomplish that project." At first, they may find your behavior peculiar, but they'll learn to love it! Everyone loves to be appreciated.

Servant leadership is authentic influence that creates value. When you influence and create value, you are leading. You may not have a leadership title, but that doesn't mean you can't have great influence and demonstrate leadership.

Make it a point to add value by sharing your ideas. Perhaps you can influence by developing systems or processes that improve work flow. See if you can equip someone with something they need to do their job more effectively. You have a wealth of talents; connect with others and serve their needs regardless of your title.

_____

_____

_____

_____

_____

_____

_____

_____

_____

_____

_____

_____

_____

_____

You've spent the last two years pouring your expertise into the employee you thought was going to become a leader within your team. She was a part of your succession plan and now she's leaving. All that development time, all that money spent on training—how can you not feel a bit resentful? Is she being ungrateful?

The truth is, servant leaders exist to develop people. We should not be looking to create versions of ourselves, but rather to develop people according to their strengths, skills, and gifts. And sometimes that means they'll leave for other opportunities. Be happy for them and feel a sense of accomplishment, knowing you've served them in an everlasting way.

Beware the org chart. As an individual contributor, mid-level manager or supervisor, are you intimidated by the organizational chart? For many years, I was afraid to "speak unless spoken to" in any encounter with a C-level leader. I think this is true in most organizations, especially those where the corporate leader is isolated physically from the rest of the group. Organizational charts are useful to show the structure of organizations and who has ultimate accountability, but that shouldn't stop you from speaking to anyone who can help you do your job well.

Next time you're in a meeting with a high-level leader or even just passing one in the hallway, speak up. Offer information of value to that person, even a simple hello. In this small way, you will spread your influence, create a relationship and perhaps add some meaning to that org chart.

Ever stop to think about the influence you have? The words you say, your body language and your behaviors all affect others—even if you're not a titled leader. When you lead with a servant leader's mindset and influence others, you will see positive change in the workplace and world.

Be intentional about influencing someone to behave as a servant leader. Maybe you can help them rethink their reaction to a situation or problem. It could be as simple as helping someone see how they can serve first. Increase your influence and change a culture.

_____

_____

_____

_____

_____

_____

_____

_____

_____

_____

_____

_____

_____

_____

_____

_____

_____

John Maxwell teaches that leadership is influence. Based on that definition, we believe everyone is a leader somewhere, sometime. Leadership isn't just about leading the band—it's also about the drummer who faithfully comes to each practice, stands in the back and provides the beat the whole band counts on.

This week, show your leadership by following the person designated as leader. Quietly use your influence to support him or her and add value to the team.

_____

_____

_____

_____

_____

_____

_____

_____

_____

_____

_____

_____

_____

_____

_____

_____

_____

_____

Listen to
Understand

Do you have a succession plan in your department? What would happen if tomorrow you won the lottery and moved to Bora Bora? Could the people you lead carry on without you? No matter the size of your team, it's wise to have a plan for the future of the group.

Listen to your team members during your one-on-one meetings. What are their hopes for the future? Take that information and what you've learned about their strengths and skills to make a succession plan. You don't need to act on it or make it public, but have it. If there are positions that currently can't be filled by anyone, note that you'll fill the vacancy from outside the group. Now that you have a plan, you can develop people in a meaningful way.

I heard a great phrase recently that I won't soon forget. Coined by Perry M. Smith, it's "squint with your ears." This phrase fits well with one of our servant leader behaviors, Listen to Understand. Listening does not come naturally to everyone, especially to extroverts. When we squint with our eyes, we're totally focused on what we're trying to see. The same should hold true if we "squint with our ears."

Focus on what people are saying to you, including accepting ideas and positive or constructive feedback. Note the emotional state of speakers and their body language. "Squint with your ears" if you really want to learn something.

_____

_____

_____

_____

_____

_____

_____

_____

_____

_____

_____

_____

_____

_____

Are you an interrupter? Are your ideas so unique and important that you simply must get them out of your mouth and into someone's ear? I speak from experience. For years, prior to working and living with servant leadership, I would often not let people finish their sentences because I couldn't wait to hear my own voice. After all, surely I must have the solution to the problem. I was fortunate. I recognized this habit in myself and started to work on being more patient.

This week, pay some attention to how you listen to understand. If you're an interrupter, slow down, and as you listen to someone, just appreciate them and their interest in what you're discussing. You'll add value to them and build trust.

_____

_____

_____

_____

_____

_____

_____

_____

_____

_____

_____

_____

_____

_____

How do you handle it when an employee makes a serious mistake? In many organizations, the tendency is to punish the employee in some way. Sometimes it's a formal punishment, or informally the employee may be treated as a risk going forward. As servant leaders, isn't it our responsibility to continue to inspire and equip in these situations?

When you are faced with an employee who has made a serious mistake, go into coaching mode. Ask open-ended questions, really listen to the person and involve them in the solution—which doesn't mean you leave them alone. Servant leaders continue to lead by supporting people in finding a resolution.

Listen to Understand—one of our nine servant leadership behaviors—seems to resonate most with our audiences. Are you truly present when people come to speak with you? Do you actively listen to your co-workers, spouse or children? Listening is a form of love, so why not spread a little of it today?

When people come to speak with you, turn away from your computer, cell phone or whatever you may be doing and look only at them. Wait for them to finish speaking before you respond. These two phrases may help you as you listen to understand: "Tell me more" and "Help me understand."

If you want an engaged team, it's important to ask for their input in decision-making. Marsha Wyrsch, executive VP for Sempra Energy, says to make good decisions, "take a listening tour" and speak to each person who may have information about the problem. Employees may have the answer. But even if they don't, they will see you care about what they think—and trust is built.

Faced with a decision this week? If you need information, "take a listening tour."

_____

_____

_____

_____

_____

_____

_____

_____

_____

_____

_____

_____

_____

_____

_____

How many times have you heard this great phrase: "It can't be done"? In our everyday interactions at work, people often use distortions like this one. They may use generalizations like, "No one really helps," or killer phrases like, "That's not our problem." As servant leaders, we need to recognize these phrases and try to show people an alternative way to think. We have talked before about non-useful beliefs and this type of language is a prime example.

Let me give you an example of how this can be addressed. Begin by really listening to people. This will help you identify the generalizations, distortions and killer phrases. Then ask questions to get more specific—who, what, when, where, which, how. Avoid asking why.

If the statement is, "It can't be done," ask, "Do you mean it can never be done?" or "If it was possible, how specifically could it be accomplished?"

Address this negative speak consistently and you will open people's minds to more positive ways of communicating and problem-solving.

_____

_____

_____

_____

_____

_____

_____

Live Your Transformation Behave the Talk™

Live your transformation is behavior number nine of the servant leader behaviors we teach. You could say it is the culmination of all the behaviors before it. The person who lives their transformation is the Level 5 leader as John Maxwell would say; the person others follow because of the person they have become. It doesn't happen overnight and it doesn't happen without great effort.

Be encouraged when you take small steps to serve first, build trust, listen to understand or any of the other behaviors. You'll see the results of living your transformation in the responses you experience from the people you influence.

_____

_____

_____

_____

_____

_____

_____

_____

_____

_____

_____

_____

_____

_____

_____

Many of us have been fortunate enough to experience truly great leadership in our lives. I know I have. When that happens, we cannot imagine working for anyone else. Unfortunately, many times things change and our leadership may change – leaving us devastated.

When and if that happens, remember the organization has a mission and purpose that should not be about one person. Once you learn to focus on the mission, it will be much easier to follow a change in leadership. Use those skills you learned under your former leader as a way to support your new leader.

_____

_____

_____

_____

_____

_____

_____

_____

_____

_____

_____

_____

_____

Beware of looking at leaders and judging them as to whether or not they are servant leaders. This can be a dangerous observation on your part. Many times the phrase, "he is not a servant leader" is used as a weapon. No one is a perfect servant leader all day, every day. Servant leadership is a process of evolution.

If you have a leader you are in conflict with and you don't feel this person is a servant leader, reflect on the following:

- **Does the individual have the desire to lead for the sake of others?**

- **Is he willing to serve first? Does he recognize his flaws and apologize when appropriate?**

- **What is your responsibility in the situation? Be willing to look at yourself before judging someone else's behavior.**

Finally, remember that assessing people by whether or not they agree with you is no indication of their intent to serve.

_____

_____

_____

_____

_____

_____

_____

_____

_____

_____

Are you serious about servant leadership? Have you allowed it to speak to your heart and mind to allow you to view the world in a different way? One of the ways to really become an effective servant leader is to let it permeate your entire life. The way you think will change and you'll look at every situation from the perspective of wanting to add value. All your relationships will be affected in a positive way.

Carry servant leadership into your personal life. Look for opportunities to serve family and friends. Try seeing things from their perspective. If you have children, serve them with no "payback" in mind. In time, magically, you'll see relationships grow richer.

_____

_____

_____

_____

_____

_____

_____

_____

_____

_____

_____

_____

_____

_____

Some time ago, I had an employee who was very upset over the size of the salary increase he'd been given. He wanted to express his frustration to management, so he came to speak with me. Unfortunately, the company was not in a position to give him a larger increase.

This employee was a genuine asset to us and he made two points that day that have stuck with me over the years.

- **He was not my direct report, but he made sure his supervisor knew he was coming to talk with me. He went over his supervisor's head, but he made sure he was honoring the authority he was put under.**

- **Although clearly frustrated, he told me he would continue to work very hard. He wanted to continue to show everyone he was a servant leader who added value—and he did.**

Are you this kind of employee?

_____

_____

_____

_____

_____

_____

_____

_____

_____

_____

There are many leadership philosophies out there. With all these ideas about how to lead, the world is still filled with disengaged, unhappy employees. We have the answer and it's been around for centuries; it's servant leadership.

Here are some tips to get started:

- **Start with your heart. Promise you will treat everyone in the organization with dignity and respect.**

- **Equip your team with everything it needs to be successful.**

- **Give the credit to others before yourself.**

- **Use courage every day because the road will not be easy.**

Servant leadership is philosophical and practical. It's not a religion and it's not soft. Follow its practices and your key performance indicators will improve. Your bottom line will improve.

Let's call this leadership philosophy what it is, practice it and change the world.

_____

_____

_____

_____

_____

_____

_____

_____

At the Servant Leadership Institute, we developed the nine behaviors of a servant leader. These behaviors are:

Serve First
Build Trust
Live Your Values
Listen to Understand
Think About Your Thinking
Add Value to Others
Demonstrate Courage
Increase Your Influence
Live Your Transformation

Rather than just having these become a lovely wall plague in your office, how about using them as behavioral expectations in our teams? Let's use them as we guide and mentor our employees. Consider making them a part of your performance appraisal system.

_____

_____

_____

_____

_____

_____

_____

_____

_____

_____

We've all heard the expression, "walk the talk." It's supposed to mean a person is being authentic and doing what he says he's going to do. We have a different term at the Servant Leadership Institute; we call it, "behave the talk.™" We believe serving others does not come naturally to most people, but if they practice servant leadership behaviors and begin to behave their talk, their mindset will change and a true servant leader will emerge.

Choose to intentionally practice one of the following: Serve First, Build Trust, Live Your Values, Listen to Understand, Think About Your Thinking, Add Value to Others, Demonstrate Courage, Increase your Influence or Live Your Transformation.

_____

_____

_____

_____

_____

_____

_____

_____

_____

_____

_____

_____

_____

_____

_____

If you are reading this book, I assume you are an aspiring servant leader. It all sounds so great—leading from your heart, inspiring and equipping your team. But every once in a while, you react to a problem or situation that leaves your team wondering how you can call yourself a servant leader. You make a mistake and your credibility takes a hit. What to do?

When you behave as less than a servant leader, ask for a little grace from your team. Be transparent enough to admit you struggle to serve like they do. If you have built relationships with those you lead, they will extend grace to you as you have to them.

_____

_____

_____

_____

_____

_____

_____

_____

_____

_____

_____

_____

_____

_____

_____

Reflection

Do you ever think about the way you think? Servant leaders do. One of the most valuable things I learned when I was trained in servant leadership was this simple question: Is my thought useful? Thinking coworkers dislike me because they don't say hi is not a useful thought. Thinking there's going to be a layoff because my manager is behind closed doors is not a useful thought.

Next time you catch yourself getting upset because you're thinking non-useful thoughts, stop and ask yourself if that thought is helping or harming you. Servant leaders learn to reframe negative thoughts. It helps them handle whatever comes their way.

_____

_____

_____

_____

_____

_____

_____

_____

_____

_____

_____

_____

_____

_____

Are your personal values in alignment with the values of your company? Oh wait—do you know what your values are? There are many of us who have never been asked about personal values, the foundational truths that anchor our lives.

Take some time to write down your five top values. They should be the things that matter most to you, the things that are non-negotiable and define your identity. Keep the list handy.

_____

_____

_____

_____

_____

_____

_____

_____

_____

_____

_____

_____

_____

_____

_____

_____

At some point in your career, you may be faced with a situation where you poured yourself into a project, only to see it abandoned by the organization because it decided to go in a different direction. This can be very difficult when you believe the project was an important one. You may be feeling deep disappointment and experience loss of trust in management. Here are some tips to move through the frustration:

- **Give yourself time and permission to be disappointed.**

- **Acknowledge the fact that you put your heart and soul into the project and that's a good thing.**

- **Share the situation with a servant leadership small group, if you have one.**

- **Speak your opinion in a professional way to your leadership and then move on to your next goal.**

- **Remember that at the end of the day, it's not about you. As a leader who serves first, you must support the goals of your organization.**

_____

_____

_____

_____

_____

_____

_____

_____

No doubt you're aware your company has a mission statement, along with a vision and purpose. But do you have one for your department? Your group will not be truly effective if you have no understanding about what your purpose is at the department level.

Take some time to think about the role your group plays within the organization as a whole. What is your purpose? When you think about fulfilling that purpose, what's the vision that appears in your mind? Write it down and share it with your team members. They'll appreciate a picture of why they do what they do.

_____

_____

_____

_____

_____

_____

_____

_____

_____

_____

_____

_____

_____

_____

Ever had people tell you you're a natural born leader? Many of us have. You keep finding yourself in that role whether it's at work or with the local parent teacher organization. But sometimes, you don't need to take a leadership role. Sometimes you add more value by being the follower. Knowing when to lead and when to follow is a skill all servant leaders should have in their toolkit.

Next time you go into a team situation, take a few minutes to think about this: will I add more value as the leader or is it time to follow? Accepting either of those roles with some thought first will lead to more successful outcomes.

_____

_____

_____

_____

_____

_____

_____

_____

_____

_____

_____

_____

_____

_____

_____

Do you ever stop and think about how you might be a better employee? I don't mean just sharpening skills you have or taking a class to improve or expand your abilities. I mean taking a look from 30,000 feet, a strategic view of how you can increase your worth and influence.

Here are three areas you can reflect on that can transform you and how you affect organizational culture.

1. **Deepen your understanding of your capability.**
   (Know your strengths.)

2. **Focus on results, i.e., positive outcomes.**
   (Eliminate non-useful beliefs.)

3. **Always seek to serve.**
   (What else can I do? How could it work better?)

_____

_____

_____

_____

_____

_____

_____

_____

_____

_____

_____

_____

Are you energized and motivated at work—or do you watch the clock constantly waiting for the end of the day so you can begin your "life"? When you feel truly energized and motivated at work, it's because you're using your strengths, talents, and competencies.

Recall a time in your life when you did something that made you feel deeply satisfied and proud. We suggest you write it down and share it with a friend. Ask your friend to point out what strengths and skills were displayed in what you did. These are the strengths you should be bringing to the work you do. As a servant leader, you are most effective when you know, use, and continually maximize the use of your strengths and talents.

_____

_____

_____

_____

_____

_____

_____

_____

_____

_____

_____

_____

_____

_____

_____

_____

How do you handle a challenging or difficult situation? Do you immediately become defensive or overly emotional? Do you feel like it's a "them or us" game? I think we all know in a perfect world, we would all be working each day for the good of the whole organization, and yet in our humanness, we can feel defensive or the need to prove our superiority. It's a terrible way to feel and a waste of time and energy.

The next time you are challenged by something or someone, take a few moments to examine your motives before you react or interact. Seek to be open, trust and look for resolution that will help the entire team.

_____

_____

_____

_____

_____

_____

_____

_____

_____

_____

_____

_____

_____

_____

_____

_____

What is your mindset when it comes to your boss? Do you think of he/she as someone who's just there to give you orders? Is he/she an ally or an adversary? And when it comes to collaboration, is he/she thought of as part of the team or part of the enemy? As a servant leader, these are important questions to consider—because you must realize leading is also about following. Your relationship with your boss is very important. You can't be a great servant leader with the people who report to you and be a lousy follower of the leadership you are placed under.

This week, take some time to really think about your attitude toward your boss. He/she may not be a servant leader, but could become one based on what he/she sees in you.

_____

_____

_____

_____

_____

_____

_____

_____

_____

_____

_____

_____

_____

_____

_____

What does the word "serve" mean to you? Does it bother you because you don't like to think of yourself being in a low position? Or, do you see it as an opportunity to help, guide or influence?

Examine your feelings about this word, because it will affect your behavior. Ask yourself how you can best serve the needs of others in the moment, in the present situation and in the long term.

_____

_____

_____

_____

_____

_____

_____

_____

_____

_____

_____

_____

_____

_____

_____

_____

_____

_____

You're so busy, aren't you? Sometimes I think busy-ness is worn like a badge of honor. You lament, "I was *so* **busy** today," when what you should be saying is, "I was *so* **effective** today!" People are increasingly stressed out and at younger and younger ages. We need to turn the tables and ask ourselves when enough is enough.

Encourage your team to take a short walk outside each day. Ask them to think about how they can add value by practicing some self-care. Servant leaders care about the whole person, so ask for their thoughts on reducing busy-ness and increasing effectiveness.

_____

_____

_____

_____

_____

_____

_____

_____

_____

_____

_____

_____

_____

_____

_____

_____

Do you find you spend more time telling people how **not** to behave than how **to behave?** No one likes to be told they don't measure up in one way or another. But if we can give our teams a more positive direction and of course model the behavior ourselves as leaders, team members will be much more open to change.

When someone you lead does something unproductive, think about the servant leader behaviors and which one could have been applied instead of the negative behavior. In your mentoring, use the behavior; describe it and give concrete examples of what a more positive outcome would look like. Give the person a positive picture of the future.

<u>Servant Leader Behaviors</u>
Serve First
Build Trust
Live Your Values
Listen to Understand
Think About Your Thinking
Add Value to Others
Demonstrate Courage
Increase Your Influence
Live Your Transformation

_____

_____

_____

_____

_____

_____

Once upon a time, a CEO who happened to be a servant leader felt he needed to mentor an employee, so he asked her to come see him. When she arrived at his door, he saw she carried a cardboard box with her. He asked what was in it. "It's my personal stuff," she replied. He probed further, asking why she had the box with her. "Well," she said, "in my past positions, if you had to go see the CEO, it meant you were going to be fired, so that's why I packed my things." This poor employee was acting based on old experiences she carried with her. How many of you react the way you do based on "old files" your brain holds onto?

This week, as you interface with people, focus on why you are feeling the way you do—especially if you are having a negative reaction. Are your feelings based on what you know to be true today or are you operating from your historical perspective?

Do you often find yourself wondering how to get what you need to be successful in your work? It's perfectly normal to think only about your wants and needs—but why not challenge yourself to think in a radically different way? What would happen if you told yourself to consistently add value in some way or another?

In every encounter you have, ask yourself how you can add value. Maybe you can pose that question to the people you meet. Keep it up long enough and other people may begin to ask the same question of their co-workers. You will experience a mindset change and become a pioneer in bringing servant leadership into your workplace.

_____

_____

_____

_____

_____

_____

_____

_____

_____

_____

_____

_____

_____

_____

The practice of servant leadership is tough; it is not for the weak of heart or head. It is vital to take the time to reflect on how you are doing as a leader at work and in your personal life. The change in your mindset cannot take place in a day or a week. As Todd Hunter, author of *Our Character at Work,* teaches, "servant leadership requires an interior renovation of the heart and soul."

Add to your calendar this week a scheduled time for reflection. It will strengthen you tremendously and help you become the non-anxious presence your team desires and deserves.

Servant leaders don't point fingers at others when problems occur. Playing the blame game is completely unproductive; it's best to look at yourself first. As the situation or circumstances are discussed, the truth will unfold. The people involved will be smart enough to see where the weak links are and plan corrections accordingly.

Do you have employees who are struggling with a project? What is your role as their servant leader? Have you equipped them to be successful? Think about it and take action if necessary.

_____

_____

_____

_____

_____

_____

_____

_____

_____

_____

_____

_____

_____

_____

_____

What kind of leader do you think you are? Are you kind, compassionate, a good listener, fair? Why not ask the people who are around you at least 40 hours a week? The kind of leader your team believes you are is vitally important to your effectiveness and success in serving them.

Ask your team to rate you on the nine behaviors of a servant leader.

_____

_____

_____

_____

_____

_____

_____

_____

_____

_____

_____

_____

_____

_____

_____

_____

_____

Appendix

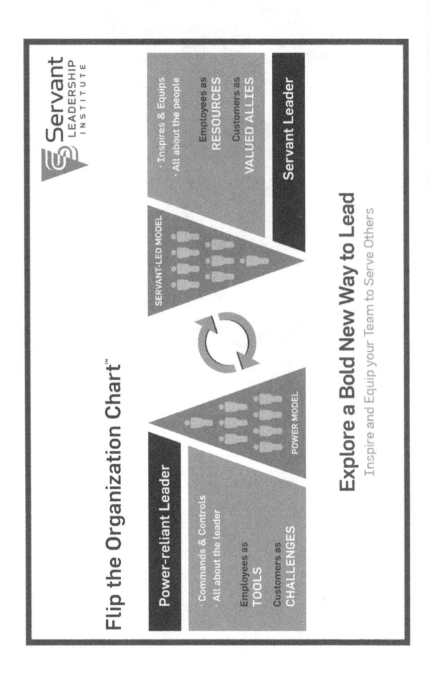

The Nine Behaviors of a Servant Leader

Servant leadership is more than a philosophy; it is a daily practice of behaviors. What are you already doing? And, what can you do better? Use this list daily to acknowledge your progress and celebrate your journey as a servant leader- a leader who is building a cohesive, trusting culture in which we can live and work.

Serve First
In each encounter, ask the question, "How can I serve you?"

Build Trust
Are you trustworthy? Are you willing to extend trust to others?

Live Your Values
What are your values? In order to live your values, you must first define them.

Listen to Understand
Do you talk more than you listen? Can you set aside all distractions and be present for people?

Think About Your Thinking
What is your attitude as a leader? Are your thoughts about yourself or others holding you back?

Add Value to Others
Are you a leader who consistently adds value? Do you always have to take the credit?

Demonstrate Courage
Are you willing to make tough decisions and follow through on them? Do you keep your commitments?

Increase Your Influence
Will you do what is right even when it may produce an unpopular outcome? Do you strive to be open and authentic with no hidden agendas?

Live Your Transformation
If you have something, do you share it? If you need something, do you ask for it?

Servant
LEADERSHIP
INSTITUTE

Contact us: (760) 707 - 3937
www.servantleadershipinstitute.com

About the Authors

Art Barter

Art Barter believes "how you get the results is more important than the results themselves." To teach people about the power of servant leadership, Art started in his own backyard by rebuilding the culture of the manufacturing company he bought in 2004, Datron World Communications. Art took Datron's traditional power-led model and turned it upside down. Together with his management team he began to serve first. The result: a small international radio manufacturer grew from a $10 million company to a $200 million company in six years. In late 2016, Datron received a record $495 million order which Art feels is a direct result of the company's servant leadership culture.

Fueled by his passion for servant leadership and the lessons learned from the implementation of Datron's culture shift, Art founded the Servant Leadership Institute (SLI) in 2008 as a vehicle to share his knowledge and to teach others how to inspire and equip those they influence.

As an authority on servant leadership implementation, Art shares his expertise in business books, on websites, through podcasts, and in articles. Currently he is a contributor to the digital magazine Forbes.com. Art is the author of *Farmer Able: A Fable About Servant Leadership Transforming Organizations And People From The Inside Out, The Servant Leadership Journal: An 18 Week Journey To Transform You and Your Organization,* and *The Art of Servant Leadership II: How You Get Results Is More Important Than the Results Themselves.*

Art was recognized in 2015 as one of the op thirty leaders named to the John C. Maxwell Leadership Awards. He has also been named by Trust Across America as one of the Top Thought Leaders In Trust for 2017, 2018, 2019, and 2020.

Carol Malinski

In 1996, Carol made the critical decision that would change the course of her life. She accepted a position at Datron World Communications, which was closer to her home and would give her more time to be with her young family. As part of the material planning team, Carol grew within the company, becoming part of the leadership team that took Datron to a $200-million company in six years.

In 2013, Carol became part of the team at the Servant Leadership Institute, making the move from material planning to writer, podcast and webinar host, and Director of Content and Curriculum. *Equip to Serve* came from her desire to share with others what she observed and learned during the last sixteen years of servant leadership practice under Art's leadership.

CPSIA information can be obtained
at www.ICGtesting.com
Printed in the USA
BVHW032251090323
660081BV00002B/449

9 781627 877619